DATE DUE

AUG 0 1 2012			
NOV 2 3 2012			
DEC 2 2 2016			

DEMCO 128-5046

Everything You Need to Know About Social Anxiety

A person with social anxiety disorder develops a fear of social situations and seeks to avoid them.

Everything You Need to Know About Social Anxiety

Lucy MacGregor

The Rosen Publishing Group, Inc.
New York

Published in 2001 by The Rosen Publishing Group, Inc.
29 East 21st Street, New York, NY 10010

Library of Congress Cataloging-in-Publication Data

MacGregor, Lucy
   Everything you need to know about social anxiety / Lucy MacGregor. — 1st ed.
      p. cm. — (Need to know library)
Includes bibliographical references and index.
   ISBN 0-8239-3324-5
  1. Anxiety in adolescence—Juvenile literature. [1. Anxiety] I. Title. II. Series.
  BF724.3.A57 R67 2000
616.85'223'00835—dc21

                                         00-010118

Manufactured in the United States of America

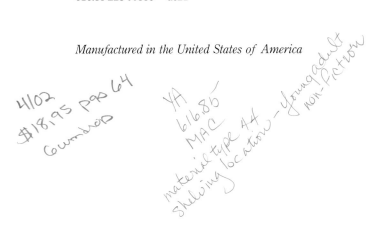

Contents

Introduction

Christie has always been very shy. As a young girl, she remembers feeling bashful when people paid attention to her. Even if someone asked her something she could answer easily—such as what her name was or her age—she felt uncomfortable sharing that kind of information. She knew that it was silly and that her discomfort didn't make much sense, but she couldn't help the way she felt.

In her teenage years, she found that her symptoms only got worse. At the age of fifteen, Christie was still uncomfortable being around people, and she felt worse about it than she had before. "When I was a young girl, people used to find it endearing or cute that I was shy," says Christie now. "Shyness is something that many people experience when they are young, but it's also something that they grow out of. Not only was the shyness still very much a part of me in my teenage years, but I also grew very anxious about my behavior. I felt silly, and a bit dumb, because I felt as though I should have grown out of the whole thing."

Christie's shyness was evident in other ways, too. Because she grew anxious about her discomfort and worried that other people thought she was abnormal or weird, Christie developed some physical symptoms when she was around people. She became so anxious in social situations that she began to stammer, feel hot, and sometimes even sweated when she was around other people.

"Every day, it seemed to get worse," says Christie. "I would feel very anxious around people even when the attention wasn't on me. And the more anxious I got, the more I thought that people would see how nervous I was. I began stammering when people asked me questions, and it became more and more difficult for me to have normal conversations with people. When the attention was on me, I just wanted to run out of the room."

It may come as a surprise to you, but Christie isn't alone. Many people have social anxiety disorder. Unfortunately, social anxiety disorder isn't talked about very often, and it doesn't receive as much attention as other disorders. There are a number of reasons for this,

People with social anxiety may experience physical symptoms when they are around other people.

including the fact that many people confuse social anxiety with simple shyness. Also, a person with social anxiety—a person who feels uncomfortable around others—is not very likely to seek help. It can be embarrassing to admit that you aren't comfortable around people or in social situations. In addition, many people with social anxiety disorder do not think that they have an actual disorder, and they often think that they are the only ones who suffer from this type of anxiety. Sufferers of social anxiety often think they are just "different" or "weird" because they aren't comfortable around others. They don't understand why it is so hard to talk to people or why they feel anxious in these situations. The fact that the people around them are able to have normal interactions with others only makes the situation worse.

As we saw with Christie, very often the symptoms of social anxiety start as feelings of shyness, discomfort, or mild nervousness. And while many people grow out of these feelings as they get older—that is, they grow out of their "childhood shyness"—those with social anxiety disorder never do. It doesn't take long before these feelings of discomfort escalate into more severe physical and emotional symptoms. Christie, for example, developed some physical symptoms such as stammering and sweating. And the way Christie felt about herself when she was in these social situations led her to feel unhappy and suffer from a lack of confidence.

As you might have guessed, sufferers of social anxiety disorder often feel paralyzed when they are in social situations. Thus the person with social anxiety disorder develops a fear of these situations, which ultimately leads to an avoidance of them. For example, if Christie felt uncomfortable and anxious at parties, she would probably be less likely to want to attend other parties in the future. And who can blame her? If she feels anxious and uncomfortable when she is around others, and gets hot, sweaty, and nervous, it makes sense that she would try to avoid the recurrence of these feelings by avoiding the situations that cause them. Unfortunately, this "cure"—that is, avoiding an upsetting situation so that she will not experience symptoms of anxiety and will not have to confront her fears—will only make her anxiety worse. The more she avoids these situations, the less comfortable she will be around people. When she finally does work up the courage to be around others, she will have even greater anxiety than before.

Luckily, social anxiety disorder is very treatable. If you or someone you know has social anxiety, this book will provide you with a strong foundation to understand the disorder and to learn about the different treatment options available. Through learning and understanding the nature of social anxiety, you will have a greater chance of overcoming it—and of living a happier, more anxiety-free life.

Chapter One

What Is Social Anxiety Disorder?

So what is social anxiety disorder? It is normal, after all, for each of us to feel nervous around others from time to time. It's normal to feel apprehension before giving a speech or to be worried about going to a party by yourself. You may get butterflies in your stomach before appearing in a play, or you may feel a little self-conscious when introduced to someone new or when answering a question in front of your class. All of these feelings are perfectly normal. It makes sense, after all, to feel nervous when you are put into a situation that you are not used to being in, or when you are worried about making a good impression on someone. We all want to be liked by others and to have others think we are smart and fun to be around. Actually, being a little nervous when you have to do these things can help you to perform better and can give you a little "nervous energy" that will keep you alert and able to think quickly.

It's normal to feel nervous when giving a speech. Social anxiety is a much more serious problem.

But social anxiety, which is also called social phobia, is much more than just shyness. It is the fear of social situations that involve interaction with other people. In other words, social anxiety disorder is the fear of being judged and evaluated by other people to the point where it is very difficult, if not impossible, to interact with others. People who suffer from social anxiety disorder fear that they are being judged negatively by others, and they worry that they might act in a way that is embarrassing or humiliating to them.

Lucy's Teenage Years

Lucy was quite outgoing and vivacious as a youngster. She always wanted to be around people and made friends easily wherever she went. So it came as quite a surprise to her parents when Lucy became a teenager and she began to withdraw and spend less and less time with them and her friends. She also seemed uncomfortable being around other people, and she used body language to show that she was not eager to talk or be talked to.

Lucy's parents were worried, but because her grades were not slipping and there were no other really troubling signs of anything serious, they thought it was just an adolescent phase that she was going through. Luckily, they were right. Lucy was going through many of the same feelings of isolation that other teenagers go through when they are growing up. One night Lucy took the initiative and asked her parents if they had any suggestions for how she could better integrate herself with the other kids at school.

With her parents' encouragement, Lucy joined some school groups that she was interested in. Instead of spending her afternoons by herself, she spent her afternoons singing in the school choir and doing some volunteer work after school. Lucy was thrilled to uncover some of her interests and to find some friends who shared them. Today, Lucy is just as outgoing and vivacious as she was as a young girl. She has many friends, likes spending time with her family, and loves to be around people.

Lucy's story is included in this book not because she suffers from social anxiety, but because she does not. True, she went through a phase of not wanting to be around people and of feeling isolated and alone. These feelings are normal for all of us from time to time. It is normal to feel different, or as if you don't fit in, or that you would sometimes prefer to spend time by yourself rather than be with others.

But if you have social anxiety disorder, it does not "clear up" on its own. Social anxiety progresses and gets worse, and does not go away without proper treatment.

If you think about Christie for a second, you will remember that along with her fear of social situations, she developed physical symptoms. She also had experienced shyness throughout her youth. Lucy, on the other hand, experienced more of a temporary discomfort with herself and with being around others. Lucy did not fear social situations, but she was going through a phase where she did not want to be in them. Whereas Christie had an actual underlying disorder, Lucy was just expressing her discomfort and confusion by withdrawing from others.

Distressing Situations for People with Social Anxiety

People who suffer from social anxiety disorder can feel distress in a number of situations. The particular situations, and the extent of the anxiety, vary with each individual. However, there are a few common situations that tend to cause anxiety in those with this disorder. These situations include:

+ Being introduced to other people. People with social anxiety disorder often feel as though others are judging them. People with social anxiety disorder might feel nervous when they are meeting someone new because they worry that they will not be liked or that they will be scrutinized carefully.

◆ Being the center of attention. People with social anxiety disorder do not like being the center of attention. Generally, it causes them to feel embarrassed and self-conscious. For that reason, people with social anxiety disorder have tremendous difficulty giving speeches and talking in front of groups of people.

◆ Being watched or observed while doing something. Because people with social anxiety disorder feel as though they are being criticized or judged negatively, they often have problems with being watched or observed while doing something. As an example, a person with this disorder might have difficulty eating or drinking in public.

◆ Meeting people in authority (important people or authority figures, such as a teacher or a boss). Any social interaction can cause a sufferer to feel anxiety; very often interactions with an authority figure can make the situation worse. A person with social anxiety desperately wants acceptance and approval from others, which can cause extreme anxiety and an inability to function.

Symptoms of Social Anxiety Disorder

Just as there are many different situations in which a person with social anxiety disorder can feel uncomfortable,

People with social phobia may be afraid of being judged when they meet someone new.

there are also a number of different symptoms that a person can experience. In addition to anxiety and nervousness, people with social anxiety disorder often feel insecure and out of place. They also tend to embarrass easily and have trouble looking others in the eyes. Other common symptoms include:

- A racing or pounding heart
- Blushing
- Dry throat and mouth
- Trembling
- Muscle twitches
- Stammering or stuttering when speaking

People with social phobia know that their anxiety is irrational and does not make sense. Nevertheless, thoughts and feelings of anxiety persist and show no signs of going away without the appropriate treatment.

Chapter Two

Two Different Types of Social Anxiety Disorder

Social anxiety disorder is often separated into two different types: the discrete type and the generalized type. The similarities and differences between the two will become clear as you read on.

The Discrete Type

In the discrete type of social anxiety disorder, the fear that is exhibited by the individual is limited to a particular situation. For example, a person with the discrete type of social anxiety disorder may be uncomfortable speaking in front of a large group of people. In other social situations, he or she may feel perfectly comfortable. For the person with the discrete type of disorder, the anxiety is relatively limited and does not appear in every social situation.

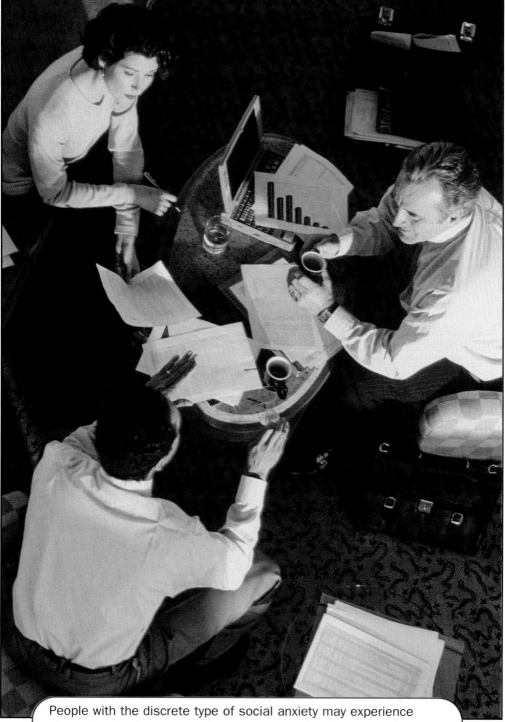

People with the discrete type of social anxiety may experience stress in situations where they are expected to interact with others.

There are several situations that typically create the most discomfort for people with this form of social anxiety. These situations include:

- Interacting at formal gatherings. A formal gathering is any situation where people are brought together for a specific reason or purpose. So, for example, a formal gathering may be a party, where the purpose is to have fun or celebrate an event or person. A formal gathering can also be something more businesslike, such as a meeting with a group of people to discuss a project. A person with the discrete form of social anxiety experiences stress when he or she is expected to interact with others, such as talking one on one or talking to a small group of people.

- Assertiveness. On the other hand, a person with the discrete form of social anxiety disorder may experience no anxiety in a formal gathering, but may feel extreme anxiety when faced with approaching strangers or other activities where assertiveness is necessary. As another example, the person with social anxiety disorder may feel perfectly comfortable at a party but very uncomfortable asking someone to do something or expressing an opinion.

♦ Being observed performing an activity. Any activity, such as eating, drinking, or writing a check, when others are around can produce a lot of anxiety for a person with the discrete form of social anxiety disorder.

If you do not suffer from social anxiety, you may regard the fears that a sufferer has as being excessive or unreasonable. It may even seem a bit silly that a person would feel nervous writing a check in a public place or experience discomfort while having a conversation with someone. As we mentioned earlier, in all these situations the fear is regarded as unreasonable even by those who experience it. A person who has excessive anxiety talking to a stranger knows that this fear is irrational and unfounded. But even knowing this isn't enough to stop the fear, and in fact it may make it worse.

Jermaine's Story

Jermaine often felt insecure and self-conscious whenever he had to speak to someone he didn't know. "It started when I was in my twenties," he says. "I always felt like the person I was speaking to was judging me and waiting for me to say something stupid or embarrassing."

As is the situation with many social phobics, Jermaine knew that his feelings made little sense.

"Of course I knew that it was ridiculous to think that people were thinking about me all the time and were having these negative thoughts toward me," he says. "I spent all this time worrying that people were noticing my nervousness and were thinking ill of me because of it. This only made me feel worse, and my anxiety got worse as well. Eventually, instead of just being a bit nervous, I began to be consumed by thoughts that other people could notice how nervous I was. As you can understand, this made it difficult for me to concentrate on what others were saying and on what was going on."

Jermaine suffers from the discrete type of social anxiety, which means that his anxiety is limited to speaking with strangers or people he doesn't know very well. He felt little or no discomfort with other social interactions, such as giving a speech or hanging out with his friends. Instead, his anxiety was more or less confined to one-on-one conversations with people he did not know. He found it difficult to concentrate and have fun talking with others because he felt as though he was being judged or evaluated. The first step in Jermaine's recovery is learning that others are not evaluating him constantly. They are just trying to get to know him and figure out what he is all about. Once Jermaine realized that people were not so concerned with what he was doing, he became much more comfortable speaking with others.

A conversation with someone he or she doesn't know may be the only source of social anxiety for a person with the discrete form of the disorder.

The Generalized Type

The more broadly defined form of social anxiety disorder is called the generalized type. The generalized type of social anxiety involves the fear of most, if not all, social situations.

As you just learned, a person who suffers from discrete social anxiety disorder experiences fear and anxiety in only one or a couple of social situations. But a person with the generalized type of social anxiety experiences fear in most or all social situations.

The generalized type of social anxiety disorder is also associated with social skills deficits. People with the generalized type of social anxiety generally report being shy much of their lives, and they tend to have relatively limited social contact with other people. As a result of their shyness and lack of social experiences, they aren't able to develop socially as well as they should. This problem becomes more obvious as their peers get more accustomed to social interactions, causing those with social anxiety disorder to feel even more distanced from their peers. As a result, their peers may tease or mistreat them, and the person with social anxiety disorder becomes extremely sensitive to all forms of rejection.

So how do those with generalized social anxiety disorder cope? Very often, they try to minimize the opportunities for negative evaluation. They do this by shunning social contact, preferring instead to be by themselves or with those they are comfortable around. They seek situations that they perceive as "safe" rather than situations where they aren't sure what might happen or who they might meet. They become reclusive.

Unfortunately, people with generalized social anxiety disorder often appear socially indifferent to others. In other words, other people may think that because they look disinterested or are quiet, that they are rude or snobbish. Of course, the opposite is generally true. People with generalized anxiety disorder often crave social involvement and acceptance from others. Unfortunately, they aren't able to express their desires appropriately, and this often gives other people the wrong impression.

Because of their stunted ability to make social contact, people with generalized social phobia tend to experience impaired performance at work or at school. They become preoccupied with the idea that others are negatively evaluating them and that they are performing poorly. Thus it becomes difficult for them to concentrate and do well at school or at work. In the world of work, having social anxiety disorder can affect the kind of job you choose. People with this type of social anxiety, for example, are more likely to choose a job that is isolated or a job where they can avoid contact with customers or other workers. Often, individuals with social anxiety disorder will work in a low paid, low skilled job, even though they are capable of a more rewarding occupation.

Ironically, people with this type of phobia often have the necessary skills to perform adequately in the feared situation. Although the person may be quite competent, they are prevented from performing well because of their negative or faulty thinking. Let's take the president of a company as an example. Rationally, the president knows that he is capable of giving a great speech. But because of his fear of speaking in front of others, he does not feel as though he will be able to do a good job. It is not as though the president isn't intelligent or isn't an appropriate speaker, but his negative thoughts are getting in the way of an anxiety-free performance. Such negative thinking is a part of both the discrete and generalized types of social anxiety disorder.

People with social phobia have also been shown to have certain biases in their thinking. More specifically, they often exaggerate the risks and dangers of certain social situations. As an example, let's say that two people are at a party. One person, let's call him Frank, has social anxiety disorder. The other, Saul, does not. Saul may have a bit of anxiety when he gets to the party because he does not know many people, but the anxiety dissipates as he introduces himself to a few people and begins to enjoy himself. Frank, on the other hand, feels tremendous anxiety a couple of days before he goes to the party, and right before he gets there, he gets very nervous. Probably without even realizing it, Frank perceives many risks or negative

Negative thinking and anticipation of negative situations is common among people with the generalized type of social anxiety disorder.

possibilities at this party. He envisions scenarios where he embarrasses himself and worries that no one will want to talk to him. So it makes sense that Frank would be extremely nervous before he heads to the party—who wouldn't be? All this negative thinking and the anticipation of negative situations makes Frank a nervous wreck. Even before he gets to the party, he wants to go home.

In many sufferers, the level of anxiety doesn't remain constant. It gets worse and worse, even over the course of a few minutes. For example, people who are fearful of speaking in small groups may start by being mildly apprehensive about their ability to find the right words to say. Next they notice their hands are trembling, their voices are quavering, or that beads of perspiration are forming on their brows. They think about how embarrassed they will become as people notice their discomfort. They become convinced that others are noticing how nervous they are. Soon their anxiety becomes severe enough that their functioning is actually impaired.

Frederick's Turning Point

"I used to have no problem attending parties and social functions," says Frederick, thirty-two years of age. "In fact, I used to love going to them, and people often told me that I was the life of the party."

Frederick's friend Louise agrees. "We were always excited when Frederick would join us at a party or social outing, like a baseball game. He was very outgoing and very funny, and he always made us laugh."

But one incident changed Frederick's outlook a bit. One night at a party, he overheard two people talking about him. They didn't like Frederick and were talking about how he always tried to get attention and often took the attention away from others. They also said that they found him annoying and that they didn't have a good time after he showed up at an event.

Sometimes a socially anxious person may compensate by trying to be the life of the party.

"Obviously, I got really upset when I heard that," says Frederick. "I began to wonder if they were right. I thought that I was just being outgoing, but then I began to think maybe it was more than that. Maybe they were right—perhaps I always had to be the center of attention. This made me evaluate my behavior, and over time I became anxious in social situations. Whereas I used to have fun meeting new people, I began to worry that I was taking attention away from someone else or was being annoying. Pretty soon, I began to avoid social interactions. It seemed much easier for me just to hang out by myself."

As in Frederick's case, sometimes an incident or experience can bring about social anxiety. However, it generally happens when a person is younger and is in a more formative stage of development. For example, some people with social anxiety disorder remember being humiliated in front of their class or being embarrassed in front of other people. Such an experience can cause a person to grow more and more anxious in social situations, eventually leading to social anxiety disorder. Incidentally, it should be mentioned that Frederick went to see a therapist about his newfound social feelings. In their discussions, it was learned that Frederick had felt very socially anxious when he was younger. However, instead of withdrawing or avoiding social interactions, Frederick responded by trying to become the life of the party. He succeeded, until he overheard that conversation at the party. Although Frederick was not conscious of it, this incident brought up a lot of old feelings that he used to experience. With the therapist's help, Frederick was able to discover where his discomfort came from and how to overcome it.

Chapter Three

Some Facts about Social Anxiety

In the introduction, we mentioned that social anxiety disorder affects many people. More specifically, social anxiety disorder affects approximately 10 to 15 percent of people at some time in their lives. The condition generally starts during the early teenage years. While most people with social phobia report having been shy for as long as they can remember, the disorder does not usually reach clinical proportions until the teenage years.

Anyone can get social anxiety disorder, and it can happen at any time, for any number of reasons. You may be surprised to learn that social phobia is the third largest health care problem in the United States. Unfortunately, it is often overlooked by educators and mental health professionals and typically goes untreated.

Possible Causes

There is no clear explanation for why some people suffer from social anxiety disorder. One theory is that social anxiety disorder is caused by a chemical imbalance in the brain. Research has shown that there may be a genetic link; that is, you might be more likely to suffer from social anxiety disorder if a close family member also has it. You may have noticed that other people in your family experience the same levels of social anxiety as you do. This can be because of genetic factors and your family environment. The family environment you grew up in, and the experiences you have had in your life, may affect the way you think about yourself and how you deal with social contact.

Sarah's Social Development

Sarah's father, Jim, is a lieutenant in the army. Because of his job, Jim and his family move frequently. Sarah is eighteen and an only child. "I have lived in nine different cities. That's a different city every two years!" says Sarah. While Sarah admits to liking the experiences she has had in these places and feels that she has learned a lot because of these travels, she also thinks that it has hindered her social development.

"I'm an only child with very busy parents," she says. "And because we move around all the time,

People with social phobia may prefer spending time alone to attending social functions.

I don't usually make too many friends." Sarah says she prefers reading and playing her guitar to attending social functions. "I've never been a part of a big social group, the kind that goes out and does lots of things together," she says. "That's okay with me, but I worry that it has stunted my relationships with people and my ability to be at ease around others." Sarah, who was diagnosed with a relatively mild form of social anxiety disorder a few months ago, thinks that her situation has led to her social anxiety. "The fact that I'm not used to being around a lot of people, and that I've always been a bit on the shy side, has led to my increasing discomfort with people," she says.

"I recently started seeing a doctor, and we have been working on strategies to decrease my anxiety. I think I'm making good progress so far." *Fortunately for Sarah, she has loving parents who stand behind her decision to seek help and are getting involved in her treatment as well.*

Because Sarah moved around so often, it was harder for her to make long lasting friendships with people. Thus her environment played a strong role in her developing social anxiety. That and the fact that she always remembers being shy—and the fact that both her parents were shy when they were young—have likely contributed to Sarah's condition. Sarah's story is in keeping with what recent research shows, that although no one knows for certain what causes social phobia, the scientific research suggests that both biological and environmental factors are probably involved.

Chapter Four

Complications of Social Anxiety Disorder

As you might imagine, there are many complications related to social anxiety disorder. The most obvious one is that you will begin to avoid certain forms of social contact. You may even find it difficult to approach your doctor to seek medical help. One of the problems with social anxiety disorder is that it often isn't recognized by others, or even by medical professionals. Many people will just perceive you as being shy. This is an inaccurate assessment, and it can have negative consequences. Imagine being told that you don't have a problem when, in fact, you do. This will make it more than likely that your disorder will go untreated.

If social anxiety disorder is left untreated, other complications can arise. You may become depressed about the effect the condition is having on your life. In fact, depression is a common effect of social anxiety disorder. People who experience feelings of anxiety around others are more likely to experience depression. Also, people with social anxiety disorder are often prompted to seek treatment only when they start to feel depressed. Often people who seek help for depression, when the cause of their depression is their anxiety, won't do so until ten to fifteen years after the onset of the anxiety.

Another complication of social anxiety disorder that is often left untreated is substance abuse. Often people begin to rely on substances like alcohol to help them deal with certain social situations that make them uncomfortable.

Pat's Lesson

Pat, who has discrete social anxiety disorder, feels extremely anxious when she has to eat or drink in public. Because Pat's job involves entertaining clients at restaurants, her anxiety makes it diffi-cult for her to enjoy herself. Although Pat isn't proud of it, she admits that she began drinking to make these situations easier.

"A few drinks helped calm me down and decreased my anxiety in restaurants," says Pat. "Unfortunately, what started off as one drink before we went to the restaurant often ended up as a few drinks during and after dinner." While Pat

Socially anxious people often rely on alcohol to help them deal with social situations.

had found a way to ease her anxiety, she realized it wasn't an appropriate cure. "As time went on, I had to face the fact that I had created a second problem for myself. On top of my social anxiety, I also had a drinking problem."

Pat summoned up the courage to seek help for her drinking and for her underlying anxiety. Now Pat is a member of Alcoholics Anonymous and is undergoing behavioral therapy for her social anxiety. "I'm not completely cured of either affliction, but I'm well on my way to getting there," says Pat. "I feel far less anxiety when I eat in restaurants with my clients, and I never touch alcohol. I feel more confident and happy than I ever have."

As we saw with Pat, substance abuse is a real problem with social anxiety disorder. You can become dependent on alcohol or drugs and make your problems worse. Ultimately it will have little effect on the underlying disorder. To treat the disorder, you must go to the root of the problem. Masking or dulling the symptoms will make your problems worse. Alcohol or drug abuse will only make treatment a much more complicated process.

It is important that you recognize the symptoms of social anxiety disorder and that you seek treatment for them. This can prevent the development of complications and will put you on the road to a speedy recovery.

Chapter Five

Treatment and Research

Today there are a number of effective options for the treatment of social anxiety disorder. These treatments can provide a remarkable improvement in behavior and a reduction of symptoms. Getting treatment for social anxiety disorder can allow you to take part in, and enjoy, the kinds of social encounters that most people take for granted. Choosing the best treatment is something that you and your doctor must discuss. Together you can come up with the treatment that is right for you.

Greg's Treatment

Greg's doctor diagnosed him with social anxiety disorder when he was twenty-five. "I can't tell you the relief I felt," he says now. "For ten years I thought I was just weird and that was why I was unable to have normal social interactions with others," he says. "It never occurred to me that it wasn't normal to have strong fears about attending parties by myself. I was so used to having negative thoughts about my social interactions with others, and I was so used to thinking of all the ways I was about to embarrass myself or say the wrong thing, that I never stopped to think that this wasn't normal."

After Greg saw a news program on social anxiety disorder, he scheduled an appointment with his doctor. Greg's doctor agreed that he probably had a form of social anxiety disorder, so they discussed treatment options. "I didn't care what the treatment was, as long as it was fast," says Greg now. "I just wanted to be rid of these negative thoughts and the uncomfortable feelings I was having each day."

Greg's doctor prescribed a medication that Greg was supposed to take every day. "Unfortunately, I had quite a few side effects from the medication," says Greg. "Very often the side effects go away after a while, but that didn't happen for me. I wasn't able to sleep, and I constantly had a dry mouth." Greg went back to his doctor and had his medication switched, all to no avail. It seemed that the medications just weren't agreeing with Greg's system.

There are a number of effective treatments for social anxiety. Your doctor or therapist can help you decide which treatment is right for you.

The next plan of action was to see a therapist. Together they worked on a number of relaxation techniques and exercises that helped Greg feel more comfortable around others. About midway through the program, Greg felt much better. "I realized that, in the end, this treatment was the right one for me. It's important not to focus too much on how 'fast' a particular treatment is going to work. It is far more important to focus on the right treatment for you."

Psychological Treatment

There are two well-known forms of psychological treatment. The first is cognitive behavioral therapy (CBT). In cognitive behavioral therapy, the therapist attempts to change the thinking processes of a patient in order to influence his or her emotions and behavior. Remember the negative thinking we mentioned before? CBT can help you change these negative thoughts and turn them into more positive ones. By focusing on your thoughts in social situations— that is, what you are thinking as you participate in social interactions—CBT can help you change the way you think about yourself and others. Your doctor will go through a number of exercises with you that will help you change the way you think about these interactions. By helping to eliminate the negative thought process, and by replacing your negative thoughts with positive ones, you will be able to think more about the task at hand, rather than focusing on what others think of you.

CBT for social phobia has been quite successful. In fact, recent research shows that after CBT, people with this problem report having a changed life, one that is no longer controlled by fear and anxiety.

The other psychological form of treatment is exposure therapy. Exposure therapy allows you to confront your fears and teaches you how to relax in anxiety-causing situations. In exposure therapy, you and your doctor will work out a program that allows you to confront your fears slowly. For example, let's say that you are afraid of going to a store, waiting in line, and buying an item. The exposure therapy for this activity would start with the first step, or going to the store and picking out the item. If that part of the exercise was successful, the next time you would do a little more of the task. So, for example, on the second day of the treatment, you might go to the store, pick out the item, and wait in line. Your doctor will teach you some relaxation techniques that you can practice as you do these steps. This will allow you to feel less anxious, and eventually you will be able to perform the exercise with little or no anxiety at all.

There is also some evidence that psychotherapy can help people with social anxiety disorder. Psychotherapy is

In exposure therapy, a patient confronts a situation, such as going to the store, that causes anxiety.

a primarily verbal means of helping troubled individuals change their thoughts, feelings, and behavior to reduce distress. The greatest advantage of psychotherapy is that the changes achieved through treatment are more likely to be permanent. However, psychotherapy requires a great deal of work on the part of the patient. In addition to weekly therapy sessions, there are homework assignments that must be completed between sessions.

Another form of treatment you might want to try is counseling. You may find that you benefit from speaking to a counselor about your condition. You can also join a support group, which would consist of other social anxiety sufferers and a counselor. Together you would perform exercises and discuss what you are feeling. Support groups exist for people with social anxiety disorder and their families, and many people find them useful.

Drug Therapy

Doctors are starting to use selective serotonin reuptake inhibitors (SSRIs) more often for the treatment of social anxiety disorder. For most patients, SSRIs have fewer side effects compared with other medications.

Although SSRIs are still being studied, they seem to be a very promising treatment for social anxiety disorder. Research is still being done regarding how these drugs work and what they work best for. So how do these drugs work? It is thought that social anxiety disorder may be due to an imbalance of a chemical called serotonin in the brain. Serotonin helps send electrical signals from one nerve cell to another. In the process, serotonin is released from one cell (the sender) and travels to the next (the receiver), where it is either absorbed or returns to the original sender cell. When a person suffers from social anxiety disorder, there may be a problem with the balance of the serotonin release system that affects the cell-to-cell communication. SSRIs may help message transmission return to normal. Treatment usually lasts for one year, but it depends on the individual patient. Other medications have been known to work in the treatment of social anxiety as well.

Unlike psychotherapy, medications require relatively little effort on the part of the patient. The big disadvantage of using medications as the primary treatment for social anxiety disorder is that, in most cases, the benefits are not permanent. In other words, when one eventually stops using the medication, the problems often come back. You and your doctor may find that a combination of therapy and medication may be the best treatment for you. If this is the route you choose to take, you would eventually be able to taper off the medication.

Chapter Six

Going to the Doctor

*J*ulia was nervous about going to the doctor. She was afraid that because she wasn't suffering from a physical problem, the doctor would think that she was just trying to get attention. "What I didn't realize," Julia says now, "is that the only person who truly knows how you feel is you. And you have to take care of yourself, which means that if something is troubling you, you should have it checked out."

When Julia met with her doctor, she told him right from the start that she felt a bit silly admitting her concerns to him. "That made me feel better right away," she says. "My doctor assured me that there was nothing to feel silly about." Julia also found that it helped to take notes while her doctor spoke to her. "My doctor told me so much *that it really helped to have notes to refer to when I got home," she says. "He even recommended some books I should read and some relaxation techniques I could try. I wrote down every word so I would be able to refer to it later."*

If you suspect that you have social anxiety disorder, the most important thing you can do is to make an appointment to see your doctor. You may be nervous or worried about what to tell the doctor, or what the doctor might think, but the most important thing to remember is that you should just relax. Remember that your doctor sees hundreds of different patients and has heard thousands of different complaints and concerns. Your doctor is there to help you, and won't judge you or think you are silly for having the concerns that you have.

Another important thing to remember is that your doctor can help you only if you tell him or her about all your symptoms and about everything you have been experiencing. It won't do you much good, for example, if you tell him or her only that you get hot and sweaty in a crowded room, or that you find it hard to make speeches. To give your doctor a complete picture of what it is that you are going through, you must make sure to list all your symptoms. Be sure to mention the situations that make you feel nervous and the types of interactions that you fear. Also tell your doctor about any physical symptoms that you may have, such as

You should provide your doctor with a complete list of your symptoms.

sweaty palms, stuttering, or a rapid heartbeat. Giving the complete description will make your doctor's job easier and your treatment more effective.

Many people find that, because they are nervous, they forget all of their symptoms and everything that they wanted to mention to the doctor. For that reason, you might want to consider writing down what you want to mention and taking a few notes with you. You might also consider bringing a pad of paper and a pen with you to the doctor's office. That way, you can take notes when your doctor talks to you.

So what will the doctor's visit be like? First, your doctor will likely talk to you about some of the symptoms you have been experiencing and how you have been feeling. He or she will ask you questions about your medical history and the medical history of your family members. Don't be concerned if the doctor asks you questions that seem unrelated to your social anxiety. Doctors like to get complete pictures of their patients, and they also use this information to rule out other possible illnesses.

Your doctor will probably do a physical exam next and run various tests as he or she deems appropriate. The most important thing to remember is that doctors are there to help you, that treatments are available, and that you don't have to suffer alone.

Glossary

anxiety   An uneasiness of mind or an abnormal sense of fear or apprehension, often marked by uncertainty about the nature of the threat.

cognitive behavioral therapy (CBT)   A therapy concerned with changing negative thoughts and certain biases that influence a person to view life in a negative way.

discrete type   A type of social anxiety where the person experiences extreme fear in only one or two types of social situations.

exposure therapy   A form of therapy that allows you to slowly confront your fears and to learn how to relax in fear-inducing situations.

generalized type   A type of social anxiety in which the person experiences anxiety and fear in all or most social situations.

phobia   An exaggerated or illogical fear of a specific situation or class of objects.

selective serotonin reuptake inhibitors (SSRIs) A class of medication that blocks serotonin and prevents it from being absorbed into the sender nerve cell. SSRIs are used as a treatment for social anxiety disorder.

serotonin   A chemical in the brain that helps send electrical signals from one nerve cell to another.

social anxiety   The fear of social situations and interaction with other people; also, the fear of being judged and evaluated by other people.

Where to Go for Help

In the United States

American Psychiatric Association
1400 K Street NW
Washington, DC 20005
(888) 357-7924
e-mail: apa@psych.org
Web site: http://www.psych.org

Anxiety Disorders Association of America
11900 Parklawn Drive, Suite 100
Rockville, MD 20852
(301) 231-9350
e-mail: AnxDis@adaa.org
Web site: http://www.adaa.org

Anxiety, Panic & Phobia Centers of New York
775 Park Avenue, Suite 155
Huntington, NY 11743
(631) 549-8867
(800) 9-PHOBIA
Web site: http://www.anxietyandpanic.com

National Institute of Mental Health
6001 Executive Boulevard, Room 8184, MSC 9663
Bethesda, MD 20892-9663
(301) 443-4513
Web site: http://www.nimh.nih.gov

In Canada

Anxiety Disorder Association of Ontario
797 Somerset Street West, Suite 14
Ottawa, ON K1R 6R3
(613) 729-6761
(877) 308-3843
e-mail: contactus@anxietyontario.com
Web site: http://www.anxietyontario.com

Anxiety Disorders Clinic
Outpatient Psychiatry, 3G
Hamilton Health Sciences Corporation
McMaster Site, 1200 Main Street West
Hamilton, ON L8N 3Z5

(905) 521-5018
e-mail: infomac@macanxiety.com
Web site: http://macanxiety.com

Internet Mental Health
601 West Broadway, Suite 902
Vancouver, BC V5Z 4C2
(604) 876-2254
e-mail: editor@mentalhealth.com
Web site: http://www.mentalhealth.com

Web Sites

Organizations
The Anxiety Network: Social Anxiety Home Page
http://www.anxietynetwork.com/sphome.html

The Anxiety-Panic Internet Resource (tAPir):
Social Anxiety
http://www.algy.com/anxiety/social

Freedom From Fear:
Anxiety and Depression Resource Organization
http://www.freedomfromfear.org/

Social Anxiety Network
http://www.social-anxiety-network.com

Social-anxiety.org
http://www.social-anxiety.org

Social Anxiety Support
http://www.socialanxietysupport.com

Social Phobia/Social Anxiety Association
http://www.socialphobia.org

Personal Experience
Fear of Humans
http://www.angelfire.com/sc/phob/index.html

Morvia's Anxiety
http://www.geocities.com/Heartland/Woods/7907/
anxiety.html

"My Gossamer Dress"
http://www.angelfire.com/me/infomaniacal/mydress.html

For Further Reading

Bourne, Edmund J. *Anxiety and Phobia Workbook.*
    New York: Fine Communication, 1997.
Carducci, Bernardo J. *Shyness: A Bold New Approach.*
    New York: HarperPerennial, 2000.
Dayhoff, Signe A. *Diagonally Parked in a Parallel
    Universe: Working Through Social Anxiety.*
    Placitas, NM: Effectiveness-Plus Publications, 2000.
Johnson, David W. *Reaching Out: Interpersonal
    Effectiveness and Self-Actualization.* Boston: Allyn
    & Bacon, Inc., 1996.
Leary, Mark R., and Robin M. Kowalski. *Social
    Anxiety.* New York: Guilford Press, 1997.
Markway, Barbara G., Cheryl N. Carmin, C. Alec Pollard,
    and Teresa Flynn. *Dying of Embarrassment: Help
    for Social Anxiety and Phobia.* Oakland: New
    Harbinger, 1992.

Marshall, John R. *Social Phobia: From Shyness to Stage Fright.* New York: Basic Books, 1994.

Peurifoy, Reneau Z. *Anxieties, Phobias, and Panic: A Step-by-Step Program for Regaining Control of Your Life.* New York: Warner Books, 1995.

Schneier, Franklin, and Lawrence Welkowitz. *The Hidden Face of Shyness: Understanding and Overcoming Social Anxiety.* New York: Avon Books, 1996.

Index

About the Author

Lucy MacGregor lives and works in Manhattan. In her spare time she writes books for young adults.

Photo Credits

Cover by Michelle Edwards; pp. 2, 8, 12, 28, 30, 43, 51 by Maura Boruchow; pp. 17, 24 by Michelle Edwards; p. 20 © Telegraph Colour Library/FPG; p. 35 © Dusty Willison/International Stock; p. 39 © Juan Silva/Image Bank; p. 46 © Uniphoto.

Layout

Danielle Goldblatt